PETER WATKINS

AS IF EVERYTHING WERE A MIRACLE

EYE WILD BOOKS
www.eyewildbooks.com

2nd Edition 2022

Published by Eye Wild Books
Green Lantern Creative LLP
1 Rose Farm Cottages
Shotley, IP9 1PH Suffolk, England, UK
www.eyewildbooks.com

Artwork and Design © Carol Lawrence
www.carollawrence.co.uk
www.instagram.com//carollawrenceartist

For my children:

Hywel, Gareth, Jevan and Gemma

Our true home is the present moment. To live in the present moment is a miracle. The miracle is not to walk on water. The miracle is to walk on the green earth in the present moment, to appreciate the peace and beauty that are available now. Peace is all around us - in the world and in nature - and within us - in our bodies and our spirits. Once we learn to touch this peace we will be healed and transformed. It is not a matter of faith; it is a matter of practice.

From Thich Nhat Hanh's, Touching Peace (1992)

CONTENTS

IN NATURE

IN NATURE

The door to the woods is the door to the temple: Mary Oliver

WALKING WITH JOHN CLARE

Each year as spring returns we walk
to a nearby spinney of hazel, oak and thorn
to which the nightingale is unfailingly drawn
and quietly stand nearby
to wait, expectant that before too long
that great songster will enchant us
with this year's virtuoso song.
And there I think of John Clare
and his spring walk to Royce wood,
where sometimes a bird would sing at
morn and eves as if it lived for song,
lost in a wilderness of listening leaves.
There to marvel that a bird of such renown
should have no better dress than russet brown
so shy a bird, so rarely seen,
unless we like Clare
drop down, concealed between
the moss green thicket trunks and wait
to see the bird in full throated song,
wings quivering in ecstasy
release the love longings
from his overflowing heart,
in his unrivalled art.

after The Nightingales Nest by John Clare

1

A KIND OF GREENING

Have you ever laid back under a mature tree,
seen the sunlight dancing in the canopy?
Someone once told me while still a young boy
that those splashes of light were
the spirits of nature dancing for joy.

And once, much later, in the grip of sadness,
I climbed high into the billowing branches
of a favourite tree, hoping those same spirits
might again dance for me; and there
in that swaying oak
felt held by another living being
of an age that I would never be;
and something else -

$\qquad\qquad\qquad$ a kind of greening.

BLACK WOOD

All that day I wandered Black Wood, a fragment
of something once vast and ancient,
following the corridors, passageways, the sudden glades,
through groves of junipers, alders, birch, cherry
and pines with reptilian bark and a spicy resinous smell.

And the only noise
The creak of boughs rubbing.

Then it started to snow,
light flakes settling on every up turned surface,
melting into it like a ghost passing through a wall.
I love old woods in snow;
realms of austere beauty and tremendous adventure,
through which wolves run,
through which Sir Gawain travels
on his quest to find the Green Knight.

'Black Wood' is a found poem. All words and lines appear in Robert
Macfarlane's The Wild Places.

WALKING WITH J A BAKER

Stepping out on a dewy morning hinting at spring,
the early sky to the east peach pink;
a thousand glinting clear white pearls hang from birch twigs;
a cobwebbed necklace decorates a footpath sign.
The fields and woods are furtive with sound.
In the far corner of a winter wheat field a kestrel,
anchored on the breeze
gracefully rocks, its wing feathers splayed,
its fanned tail making minor adjustments to its position,
its sharp eyes - with twice the visual acuity of the human eye -
tracking some movement below.
I walk on past Bylam Wood where buzzards
nested last summer in a twig tangled tree fork eyrie,
then set off south towards the river.
I hear them first, mewing urgently,
then see a pair spiralling high over the fields
majestically soaring like gods;
their pale patterned golden brown wings -
the span of outstretched arms,
glow in the morning sun.
The male suddenly plummets, twisting, turning, tumbling -
soars again, then repeats its aerobatic courtship display.
Feeding pigeons see it too
and race for the cover of Boleyn Copse;
irritated by the commotion rooks scold, stir and rise from the
stubbled field.

On a field track a neat pile of pigeon feathers,
a recent sparrowhawk kill.
As I look on a breeze scatters the feathers, some fly into the air
as if the spirit of the dead bird was trying to reclaim them.

J. A. Baker (1926 - 1987) was an Essex naturalist & nature writer. His
books 'The Peregrine' and 'The Hill of Summer' are now widely
acclaimed for there acute observation and poetic prose.

THE SHAPE SHIFTER

He or she (how do you sex a robin?),
appeared one morning on the kitchen doorstep
demanding to be fed.
Now a regular visitor
she - let's call her she -
fixes me daily
with a fierce eye -
I say fierce -
It is not a kindly eye, but
we're working on it -
this connection of ours.
She brings the excitement,
I bring the meal worms.
That's where it stands at the moment.

She has so much to teach,
she knows the wild world
from which I am so alienated.
It's simpler, harder,
it's about living,
which is more than survival.

Sometimes she sings just for the pleasure of singing.
Sometimes she flits about the garden
just for the hell of it.

Anyway, this is what she's told me,
so far!

SNOWDROPS

Pushing up through the iron clad earth
this year's snowdrops;
their white bell heads
drooping in supplication
to greet the God of spring,
opening to reveal their purity and grace,
delicate dabs of green, at petal ends,
almost unseen,
put there with the fine tip
of a divine brush,
while into the hush of the day
a watchful robin
pipes an ice sharp melody
in salutation to the awakening earth,
uplifting our wintering hearts with gladness.

Is not sight a jewel?
Is not hearing a treasure?
Is not speech a glory?
Pardon my dullness who am not alive to this gift.

After Thomas Traherne (1636 - 74)

SEED

In darkness
the seed lays waiting,
sometimes for years, and
holds fast to its dream of what it may become.
It waits
for the kiss of the wet warm earth
to rouse it from its sleep;
then from its husk a resolute shoot
pushes through
the giving soil seeking light.
In time the delicate petal head
a miracle of red unfurls and adorns
the stem,
seducing passing pollinators
into its intimate folds,
where renewal begins again.

THE SHELL LINE

The white bright whelk shells,
impossibly sculptured, all in a row,
wind down the broad expanse of the wave blasted
brown pebble beach to the lip
of the shingle bank,
stopping short of the voracious -
but now calm, sea.
All have been lovingly laid there,
any breaks repaired by those that pass.
The story they tell is of healing,
is of hope,
is of peace,
and the strong life force,
wild and free
that calls us to such places..

Shingle Street Suffolk

THE EDGELANDS

The summer bank huddles between field and garden,
edgeland beyond the reach of herbicidal mists and verge cutters.
Plants jostle for space in wild profusion.
Like all wild things driven to the edges,
holding on, holding on,
to this small, giving
patch of earth.
Insects busily skitter,
finches drop down,
seclusive slow worms
and elusive lizards find shelter in the leaf litter.

The thought comes: what of our own wild selves,
driven to the edgelands?

A prayer utters itself:
Oh may the feral angel of our natures
Live on the edge of reason,
elemental, passionate, soulful; desiring life.

RUNNING IN EARLY SPRING

It is a bright blue sky day -
The sun has penetrating warmth -
The earth is waking -
Horses in a paddocked field stir -
A spirited chestnut mare kicks up
And races along the paddock fence.

I'm following the sinewy lanes that hug the estuary.
You can feel the earth stirring -
Primroses decorate the hedgerows -
The celandines shine
as if particles of sun
had showered the banks -
A great spotted woodpecker drums on a dead tree -
Lapwings cluster on the fields
and above a nearby copse buzzards spiral.

Thrilled by this moment
my heart kicks up and races away
taking me with it.

EVENING BLACKBIRD

Every evening
throughout June
a blackbird
serenaded us from the topmost
branches of the hawthorn tree.
A melody so full of virtuosity
that stilled by the sound,
we who heard it
could only listen and be glad.
It was his last song of the summer.
As June passed into July
he no longer sang.

Perhaps it was territorial,
But my gladdened heart tells me –
and I could be wrong –
that he was proclaiming,
in his own sweet way,
nothing but the joy of song.

FOREST CLEARING

Sitting in the middle of a wood in dappled light,
just breathing, each cell oscillating with green healing energy,
sensing the sentient presence of ancient pines
standing erect –
(I want to say through everything)
observing me benignly,
securely rooted,
(as I too at this moment feel rooted),
in the mothering earth.

Who knows what they think!
Their greenly gleaming canopy
reaching skyward, hungry for the light.
The breeze humming hallelujahs through their fine needles.

How can I not feel gratitude for such a moment!

LET A POEM BE A SIGH

Sometimes words cannot be found
to carry the
fulsomeness
of the hearts attending.
What sights we may see,
what sounds we may hear,
In this hallowed world:

How the leaves shine -
How the fields shimmer -
How the heather glows -
How the water gleams -
How the very rocks
could at any moment burst into flame
from remembrance of heat.

If we could only see
that emanating light
streaming from all things,
In wide eyed astonishment
we would sigh in joy.

SPRING VIOLETS

I want to turn each new day like a weather-vane
to the breath of the divine;
let it point in the direction of love.
Let me live lovingly;
let me be soulfully alive.

In truth I am often dulled in spirit.
But today the purple violets
peppering the grass seem somehow sacramental;
each single tiny petal head
a microcosm of beauty & goodness.
I prostrate myself on the damp earth
to be intimately in their presence,
noticing for the first time
the shaft of gold at their centre.
And have you ever in your life
seen such a perfect heart shaped leaf?

THE FIRST FLOWERS

Have you ever thought of the first flowers?
Imagine!
They arrived long before humankind
and covered the earth.
Imagine that!

Have you ever wondered what they might be here for?
I thought I might enquire,
as today the hedgerows, banks and fields are alive with bloom:
the honeysuckle, the dog rose, the buttercup,
the bee orchid, the field poppies the ox-eye daisies.
All of them know.

You have to spend time.
They're busy; they have important work to do.
A dog rose won't say anything if you're impatient.
After a time, attentively in their presence,
this is what they said:
We are a gift from the realms of beauty and goodness;
we bring joy to the world;
we want you to love life.
Believe me
That's quite a lot for a dog rose to say;
they are usually so unassuming.

SOMETIMES WE ARE LIKE THIS

Every morning a gang of starlings
in their spangled vests of greens
and blues and purple,
their stiletto beaks ever ready,
visit the garden.
They fight and squabble amongst themselves
whistling, clicking, squawking, squealing,
take what's on offer and move on.

After the commotion the garden settles.
Today one bird remains sitting alone on the fence
attending to its plumage,
its colours iridescent in the morning sun,
quietly burbling, in the way they do,
like something said under your breath.
I didn't catch it all but it was something like:
this is who we are, love us if you can.
We are also the whirl
and swoop and swirl of the shape shifting clouds
that mesmerise and delight your eye in a winter sky;
who then, of one mind, disappear.

SOME STONE STORIES I WAS ONCE TOLD

1.

How this black, sea smooth, oval pebble
had once been near to the summit
of a majestic mountain,
part of the peak,
but had become dislodged,
rolled down into a river and
from there carried to the sea.
Eventually, after many years,
it was washed up on this beach.
How it remembered its mountain realm
and dreamed of someday returning.

2.

How these tiny white, almost translucent, pebbles
were the fossilised tears of a beautiful mermaid,
imprisoned inland by an evil enchantress.
How unable to return to her beloved marine world
she cried every day for ten years
until her salty tears formed into an ocean and she escaped.
How if you collected ten fossilised tears
love will always return to your life.

3.
How stones with holes, holey stones, (perhaps Holy),
kept you safe from harm.
How there was once a great pestilence that
threatened to wipe out the human race.
The ancient gods because of their love of humankind
made them as keep-safes and
scattered them on beaches for people to find.

Of course I believed the stories.
Why wouldn't you?
Here is the black pebble, still waiting.
Here are ten white teardrops in a velvet pouch.
Here is my necklace of Holy stone.

THIS IS WHAT THEY SAID

I am practised (though far from perfect)
in the art of doing nothing;
Just being alive in the world, fully present
to that one precious moment;
and it is not easy.
So used are we to hurrying on,
hurrying on to the next bit of living
that we forget to live now.

I was standing on a rise at a field's edge
looking down at a sun spangled estuary,
tasting the fresh sea breeze,
when out of the corner of my eye, I saw,
a hedge away,
two roe deer,
quizzically observing me,
and although fleeting,
(they bounded away, as they usually do).
It felt to me like a meeting.

Later I imagine them telling the herd
in what ever way they might do that:
We saw a human today.
What were they doing?
Nothing, just standing -
just looking -
just listening -
just smelling the air.

What was their intent?
Just being, just belonging,
to this astonishing world.

I WOULDN'T DOUBT IT FOR A MOMENT

Maybe you, like me, find something magical
in an ancient wood -
Especially in May -
in dappled sunlight -
when the wood is greening -
when the heart song of birds is given full throat -
and the woodland floor a coverlet of bluebells.
It is alive with energies;
as if the old tales still reside there,
as if some enchantment
still inhabits the glades.

Imagine, if in the heart of such places
you encountered some wise,
benevolent, elemental being,
who might tell you the truth of your life.
Perhaps you have?
I wouldn't doubt it for a moment.
And if you had asked,
what is the meaning and purpose of my life
and the answer came: love is the meaning;
love is the purpose.
I wouldn't doubt it for a moment.

CALLING US HOME

The footpath runs diagonally
(it knows where it's going)
across a blue green wheat field,
today rippling in the breeze
as if a giant hand had caressed it,
the grain heads waiting for the
swelling rain and the
alchemy of a summer sun.
The field is studded with poppies,
like crimson paint splatters,
and the silver song of skylarks
distils joy in the heaviest heart.

At a certain point an expansive view
of the river opens up,
today like plate glass,
stopping us – as it always does, in our tracks.
At such moments there is nothing but the landscape;
You take it in (or it takes you in)
a kind of glorious oneness; a lover's embrace.

Is this how a place, little by little,
enters our hearts,
creates that deep sense of belonging,
or longing?
Is this how a certain place, a patch of land,
becomes part of us and we part of it?
We carry it everywhere
and always it is calling us home.

SMALL SONG FOR PRIVATE CLARKE

Private Clarke died in anonymity,
on an asylum ward at seventy three
shrapnel still embedded in his skull -
a souvenir from Ypres
and half healed wounds
much deeper still, that held his life
captive in fearfulness and strife.

No diaries or poignant letters home exist
to tell the tale of his unspeakable war;
except - a gardener before
he gathered plants and seeds
from abandoned village plots
and on the lips of trenches planted
gardens of ox-eyes, marigolds and forget-me -nots.

On seeing those familiar blooms
rise in quivering beauty amidst such desolation,
every man took heart,
every man was strengthened to his station.

SHE LOVES ME SHE LOVES ME NOT

While wandering today,
finding myself enchanted, as when a child,
by the seed heads of dandelions,
abundant on the field track;
and turning,
as might the heart's compass
seeking the presence of an absent love, I blow:
she loves me, she loves me not,
she loves me -
each breath launching plumes of seeded parachutes
on their breeze blown journey near and far
to where that love might be.

Perfection belongs to the Gods;
but tell me,
doesn't the magnificence of that silver white sphere
fill you with astonishment;
wonder even?

THE GARDEN (A Villanelle)

Let us with mindfulness attend the garden of our days,
in nurtured ground the succoured spirit thrives;
may blessed fruitfulness be the measure of life's ways.

The tended plot on which at ease we gaze,
from which the many seeds of hope and promise will arise;
Let us with mindfulness attend the garden of our days.

Green fuse will through the hardest clod upraise
the shoots and stems of blooms delighting dullest eyes;
May blessed fruitfulness be the measure of life's ways.

When gardens full of colour and abundance blaze,
the sorrowful spirit soars and soon revives;
Let us with mindfulness attend the garden of our days

Nature in full glory does amaze,
its many gifts with heart and soul we prize;
May blessed fruitfulness be the measure of life's ways

Within us bounteous nature seeks to raise
the finer feeling that life's darkest trials defies;
let us with mindfulness attend the garden of our days;
May blessed fruitfulness be the measure of life's ways.

OH WONDEROUS ONE

Having walked in summer heat I rest
supine in meadow grass,
amongst the spikelets and spears,
deep and unseen,
their plumed seed heads
wafting in the breeze above me.
(I'm sorry I do not know your names
oh beloved grasses that offer me this bed of green).

Dozing in my grass cradle
an orange-tip skitters its way on to my arm,
bare skin offering a landing ground, to rest,
to warm its delicate white wavering wings;
its twitching antennae perhaps sensing
some unspecified life form, unaccountably
nestling amongst the grasses;
It's proboscis sampling droplets of sweat
pooling in the crook of my arm.
(And may I say oh wondrous one,
how happy I am to share my body fluid
with such a dazzling creature).

AS IF EVERYTHING WERE A MIRACLE

Today the garden seed heads catch my eye.
I do not know of many things
as magnificent as a seed head;
A miracle of nature's design.
The sunflower,
the allium,
the poppy,
the exotic love in a mist -
countless others
containing
the mystery of becoming
all they may be;
first in darkness
then in the light of the world,
unfolding such form,
such colour,
playing their part in the scheme of things.

The world has taken this time
to open my dulled eyes;
I live now as if everything were a miracle.

IN PRAISE OF SLOW

I like to start my day slowly
and then get slower.
Best of all I like to be still,
just looking, just listening,
allowing all thoughts to be carried away,
to let them go,
to be emptied,
to leave room to be fully alive in this hallowed world.
It's like a meditation
but really
it's just breathing,
just being;
I would say just witnessing.

If you don't mind me asking:
When did you last watch
a bumblebee reverse out of a foxglove;
or for that matter when did a red admiral
sunning itself on a path somewhere
leave you wondering when you last
saw anything of matching beauty?
When did the soft glow of an evening light on a field
last hold you enthralled?

You may well ask
when did everything become so sacramental..

AFTER WATCHING DAVID ATTENBOROUGH

Crawling along the bedroom sill
on six fine legs –
antennae sensing the territory, a beetle,
with a fine green iridescent back.
How it came to be there I don't know -
it has no wings and although its legs are fine,
they are not jumping legs.
Pardon me who knows so little -
I don't know your name;
I don't know your purpose in the world.

Don't we all have a purpose?

For all I know it might be endangered
and without its presence
a whole strata of life could collapse.
Imagine having a life of such significance
that a whole ecosystem depended on you;
a creature infinitely
more important than this one human being
who despoils things,
who doesn't have six fine legs
or a beautiful iridescent back;
who can only patch together a few words like this.

A LOVE TOKEN

When I walk the field ways, river paths, the woodland tracks,
I like to walk alone; elementally.
I like to feel my body moving through space,
feel the estuary breeze lightly touch my skin.
I like my eyes to be captured by
bees feeding urgently on the autumn ivy;
the purple-blue glow of sloes in the blackthorn hedge;
or the shine of ripe red rose hips.
I like my ear to be drawn by the calling of nearby rooks,
or the mewing of buzzards above a copse.
Most of all I like the feeling of being alive,
breathing with all of nature,
and sometimes too that quiet, insistent voice,
reminding and reminding again:
you too are part of this magnificence.
In those moments if I could sparkle
like the river on this bright fall day,
I most surely would.

If you have ever walked with me
It would have been a token of love.

A GIFT UNBIDDEN

Walking today,
heart heavy, disquieted.
Maybe you know such days
How they can descend on your life,
or perhaps ascend
from some dark region
of your inner world?
And if we are wise we stay with it;
let dark be dark.

But sometimes, as for me this day,
we need consolation, something transcendent;
sometimes we need a presence,
something to strengthen the spirit;
and so walking today, a gift unbidden:
a clutch of ringed plover chicks
the colour of pebbles, almost unseen,
scurry away along the estuary shore
to the safety of their mother's wings.

IN CONTEMPLATION

Our real journey in life is interior; it is a matter of growth, of deepening, of an ever greater surrender to the creative action of love and grace in our hearts. Thomas Merton

EARLY ONE MORNING

It is early and I'm awake.
The sun is also rising
and spreading a red flush
on the rim of the earth to the east.
A blackbird sits on the garage roof
its sharp eyes looking eastward
waiting to herald the gift of a new day with song.
Lord open thou my lips
and my mouth shall show forth thy praise.

There is a hush -
an expectation?

In some beatific moments like these we
hold our breath as if to arrest time.
Now I breathe out with a long sigh
that might be a prayer.

UNITY

What does it mean to be at one with all creation?

All forms flow into being
with God's grace,
their collected atoms singing in wonder and thanksgiving
at the unfolding of this mystery.

The hills, their peaks reaching heavenward,
know such things from the clouds,
the clouds know such things from the stars,
the stars know such things from the assembled host
and tell of it in their pulsing, shimmering light.

Were you like me, always too busy hurrying on
to the next piece of living to hear?
Yet in the cave of our hearts we too know such things.

ROCK CHAPEL

It was like a blessing given
to be there alone in that tiny chapel,
embraced by the softly glowing
light of the stained glass.

Anchor me in your blue peacefulness,
warm me with soft yellow,
enliven me with your reds,
rest me in your tranquil green.
And I sang into the resonant silence in gratitude,
quietly at first,
then with more passion:
"Amazing grace how sweet the sound",
and the glass glowed the more, so that
all the colours were sound and all
the sound colours
that blended and merged into
white light and blessed melody.

Rock Chapel, St Beuno's Jesuit Spirituality Centre, St Asaph.

A DAILY JUBILATION

The morning sun
has crept over the eastern horizon,
eased in through the curtains,
entered my closed eyes
and stirred me from sleep.

A robin is perched on the garden table
looking in at me looking out.
The bird feeders are already busy:
starlings muscle in,
goldfinches flit,
greenfinches wait,
blue tits swing acrobatically
and sparrows sing a daily jubilation
from the hedge.

If a poem can be a prayer
I want it to give thanks for the ordinary miracles of life.
To wake, to be greeted by these feathered beings is a daily gift.
What would the world be without birdsong?

Hello my friends.
Morning to you
my cheerful companions.
How can I be downcast
when all my garden birds are saying:
this is another God given day - live,
live hopefully.

A SIMPLER LIFE

I've often thought wistfully,
of a simpler life;
a secluded dwelling, a chance for solitude,
a sidestep from this frenetic, noise filled world;
from this attritional, acquisitive way of living.

I've often wished longingly,
to cast off all addictions,
to live mindfully and vitally:
to walk with awareness,
sit in contemplation,
work with gladness,
seeing them all as blessings
and come to feel,
the joyful and resolute pulse of life.

For far too long regretfully.

TRUTH

I want to write about truth.
Not the testaments of invention
with which we author our lives;
not the outright lies we tell, half believing;
but the truth of who we truly are.

How often we strangle at birth
that which is most real in us,
to please, to conform,
to present a face to the world.
How over time the real gets buried
deeper and deeper still, out of sight
till eventually it cannot be resurrected
and restored to the light.

How we grieve this loss so great.
How we must grieve.
For beyond the sorrow is the True Self,
which like the cycle of the moon is
first a sliver of pale light in the night sky
then shines full and magnificent
in the canopy of our lives.

FOR ONE WHO IS SORROWFUL - A BLESSING

There are many heartaches in this life.
Sometimes unattended griefs accumulate;
with weariness the spirit endures,
but at some point they will fall in on the mind
and take you down.
You cannot force yourself back into life
There is nothing else to do but
allow the sorrows to take us where they will -
we have to dwell there,
the unwept tears will come,
the anguish will scour your heart.
Be kind to yourself; in time
your soul will reclaim you.
You will notice again the small miracles of life:
how the gleaming motile droplets of rain
trace a path down the window pane;
how the soft glow of light on an evening field soothes;
how the silence cradles you;
how the touch of a stone
resting in the palm of your hand, calms;
how the gentle ripples of a slow river
whispers a teaching of peace;
how the sea birds wheel and glide with freedom and ease,
at home in their aerial world;
how life goes on unfolding,
calling to your yearning heart, come, come,
you are part of this,
you are part of this.

AND THEN AT THE LAST

And then,
after life's exquisite cavalcade has passed,
a deep intake of breath,
the last,
the kind we take before
going deeper and deeper still
into that great mystery that awaits us all.
Then the last out-breath,
like a long sigh,
before relinquishing our hold on life,
letting go,
drifting away,
into that unknown land;
a searching dove,
leaving -
blessings be -
a legacy of a life well lived,
a legacy of love.

TELL ME IF I'M WRONG

But are we not creatures of the light.
Do we not feel a familiar joyfulness
as the earth spins & tilts towards
our own dear star.
The light returns;
minutes are added to minutes
and we cast off our wintering ways.

Tell me if I'm wrong,
but don't you feel it enter your body
warm & glowing;
don't you, like the leaf buds
holding a green newness,
feel yourself unfurl.
Don't you feel yourself shining?

DANCE ME TO THE END OF DAYS

Surely the body was made to dance.
These marvellous bodies in their youthful vigour,
in their ageing grace,
speaking their truth, in their strength, in their vulnerability,
in their sensuality, in their passion, in their joy, in their sorrow -
in their sheer aliveness.
How I would leap if I could, how I would spin if I could.
Let's give praise in shape;
celebrate the expressiveness of the body,
most beautiful and wonderful in its form.

Let me O great dance master
be responsive to this wild beating heart,
let me feel the zing in every nerve ending,
every muscle fibre;
grant me zest for this one precious life
and dance me to the end of days.

Then at the last a deep bow.

LET DARK BE DARK

I am one acquainted
with the wild edge of sorrow.
This is what I know of that place;
It is not much,
but it is something.

What we love we lose;
but who would not wish to love?
Those dear to us, yes,
the joys & fulfilments of our days, yes, yes
and what of those now hazy visions
of all we might have been
in a life less circumscribed,
before we settled for less;
so much less.
And our own mortal lives so brief, so precious.
But oh my, oh my
how we neglect the sorrowful heart
how we try all ways to dull the pain.

Let dark be dark.
It is not to be feared,
though at times we feel we might be lost.
In the darkness the soul awakens;
we return (eventually) with such gifts:
gratitude, compassion, joy; and we love again,
astonished that such a life is possible
for one fallible heart -wrecked human being.

SOMEONE SINGING

It is early.
Someone is singing
on the estuary shore
this quiet winter morning.
Not showily,
but softly,
and, I think, joyfully.

The sun is up
after days of rain
and has turned the river
into polished pewter.
Everything gleams in gratitude.

I turn and look,
expecting to see
the happy soul singer,
but then I realise
to my surprise,
the singer is me.

INTO GREAT SILENCE

Often, in an empty church,
embraced by the silence
I hear, in the quiet depths of that space,
the faint echo of songs sung,
liturgy intoned, prayers spoken over centuries,
now in some inexplicable way embedded
in the fabric of that place.

Often, in the landscape too,
walking alone along meandering paths,
there is that faint footfall,
ancestral voices, whispers on the breeze
of those long since dead:
Brother we too walked this way;
and did you notice the sweet song of the larks,
the hares leap and run,
and the slow wings of the heron overhead.

ON WALKING BESIDE STILL WATERS (April 2020)

In dark times
we must take what ever light we can hold
and shine it into the darkness.
Let us not be afraid.
Let us rest in the goodness of the world.
Let us draw close to each other,
trusting, sure,
that in these perilous times,
heart reaching out to heart
will find there the courage to endure.

SOME SAY (In a time of pandemic)

Some say
it is an upwelling of wisdom from the earth,
taking in hand a troublesome species.

Some say
all this despoilment
required some response.

Some say
We have to transform ourselves,
nothing less.
It is the sacred task
we who live at this moment have been given.

Some say
It can only be accomplished through love;
love for all beings, love for this astonishing world.

AFTER THE STORM

Sometimes a storm blows in
seen or unforeseen
and changes the landscape of our lives.
What was ordered becomes disordered,
leaving us bewildered, fearful, bereaved.
How could it be, we sigh, that our familiar lives
could be swept away in the blink of an eye.
At times like these we need safe harbour
we need to hold on,
find the strengths that anchor us,
pray if we can.

Sometimes it takes a wild wind
to take apart our lives
so that it may be built anew.
Chaos too is part of our story,
we children of the universe.
What are these green shoots -
we might say in amazement,
pushing up into our devastation.
They are our duty to life:
to live, to love well, to live better.

MAY WEDDING (A Blessing)

May blossom frothy on every bough
We gather here to witness these hearts interlace,
Giving themselves in mystical union they vow
To love, honour and cherish, one to another, with godly grace.

Though those ancient vows may not be said, yet
Meant they are, and blessed you are just the same,
The ritual of rings exchanged is sacrament enough (lest we forget),
An act igniting love's enduring flame.

And if life's darkest hours should test those joys
That now you find in loving company,
May love from other realms, which providence employs,
Bring comfort and restore your harmony.

May these blessings given allay life's care
May you forever walk on happy air.

For Gemma and Rob

I IMAGINE SOME GOOD WILL COME

As a child, each evening,
kneeling at the bedside before sleep
I was taught to pray:
A blessing on my family, each in turn,
and finally, bless me O Lord and make me good.

I gave up on prayers many years back.
What good did they ever do anyway?
Now late in life, unaccountably,
I have started praying again:
God bless and keep all those who suffer,
God bless and keep all beings and this precious earth.
See what a burden my prayers carry now!
I imagine them flying off in all directions;
I imagine they are always heard;
I imagine some good will come of them.

Sometimes I pray without praying,
prayers of gratitude -
it is something like a stirring of the heart
in the presence of beauty, in nature,
on seeing dear friends, in acts of love.

VESSEL

1.
I cup my hands to receive
the cool clear water from the well and drink,
it tastes of rock and earth,
of purity and goodness,
and for a moment
the vessel holding it
is as holy as a communion cup.

2.
We begin in the pouch of the womb;
anchored in this aqueous world
cells differentiate and grow:
skin, bone, heart, nerves;
a vessel like no other,
holding the mystery and the miracle
of our becoming.

3.
Marvellous heart; in a lifetime
beating more times than we can imagine;
each beat sending blood to the lungs,
returning bright with oxygen;
each pulse a surging life sustaining flow
of nourishment to every single body cell.
Amazing heart; keeper of wisdom.

4.

The simple Saxon cremation urn
sits on display in a glass case at the museum;
beside it a bone comb & glass beads;
Its runic inscription denotes, we are told, a female;
once, with such heartache, tenderly laid in the earth.
Woman with combed hair, wearer of beads,
I want to bless you for your life.

5.

The singing bowl, perfectly proportioned,
sits waiting in the palm of the hand.
It is a vessel of sound, that once struck, rings -
some might say, a transcendent note,
that resonates in the body,
some might say with the soul,
inviting you into an awareness of that other reality.

IT IS SOMETHING LIKE THAT

It is woven into the fabric of life;
all that live experience adversity.
We cannot claim a smooth passage as our right;
and yes, sometimes it is terrible,
and sometimes it seems unjust,
the suffering endemic in the world.
Perhaps it has touched your life too?

How can we bear it?
Where do we find solace; where do we find
the grace to accept and endure;
the courage and strength to come through?
It might simply be a hand held, a smile,
some softly spoken words,
a quietly loving presence.
Think how the early crocus
dispels the bleakest of winters.
It is something like that.

WHY OH WHY LORD DOES IT TAKE SO LONG

There are dark days
when I seem as far from goodness
as I ever was;
as distant from the selfless self -
that simply wants to live, love and
laugh like a Buddha,
as I've ever been.

Why oh why Lord does it take so long?

Then I walk.
Any walk can be a pilgrimage;
It is not where you are going
but why you set out;
there is always a question to be asked
even though it might not be fully known;
If we listen an answer may come anyway.
On this day as I walk, a teaching:
Let dark be dark, how else
can we see where the light of a
kinder future is streaming from.

WHAT IF THIS IS WHY WE WAKE

Do you ever wake
thanking God -
whatever that might mean to you,
for another day?
Do you ever wake with a sense of gratitude
that life has given you another light filled day
to be part of this astonishing world?
And do you ever feel that comes with a duty
to honour and make the most of this gift?
Do you ever wonder what that honouring might be?
The birds sing, the trees leaf, the river flows;
what are we to do with this one precious life?
Did you ever think we might be here for love,
for all people, for all other beings,
for this beautiful blue planet?
What if this was why we wake every morning;
It would change everything wouldn't it?

I ASKED MY COMPANION

I asked my companion if she was happy,
she laughs and smiles a lot.
She said yes;
It's deep inside.
I am happy too -
sometimes;
though I often wear a serious look;
I smile inside, my eyes smile too -
sometimes.
My mouth has never quite mastered the expression.
I have a sadness;
it's deep inside.
There is so much suffering in the world,
So much to feel outraged by,
so much to feel anxious and despairing about.
But then again
there is more goodness in the world than we can ever know;
at this very moment
a thousand selfless acts of love are taking place;
sometimes I can almost feel my mouth wanting to break out.

LET LESS BE MORE

If we are wise we move towards a state of being where things that once mattered, matter less. Call it getting older if you must, but I like to think It is the unfolding of something truer and deeper, in our nature. What I notice is achievement is less important, material things too. It doesn't matter now that there are so many things I don't know, things I haven't done, places I haven't been. Less need now for approbation, for self deception, for self-centredness. To let go of these preoccupations (why has it taken a lifetime?) offers so much more space, more time, to live mindfully, peacefully, letting only what matters matter. And doesn't it strike you as extraordinary to be here, now, at this moment, part of creation, loving what we love: those dear to us, all beings, this extraordinary blue planet? Don't you feel the swell of gratitude?

SHOW ME OH GREAT ONE (2020)

Is it simply an accident of time
that we are here now,
living at this moment of crisis and chaos;
a time when so much is wrong with the world
and the very survival of all beings is threatened.
Or is it, do you think, we are here now
to receive a cosmic lesson in sacred duty,
to hear a call to transformation,
to bring forth our finer feelings,
to release the good embedded in the heart of humanity,
to heal, to co-create the world anew?
What if this were indeed our great work.
Do you like me feel it calling?
Show me O great One what I must do.

WHERE WORDS FAIL MUSIC SPEAKS

How is that music expresses all
that is in the human heart?
I don't know, I am just amazed
how it speaks to me so eloquently
of love, of sorrow, of joy;
how its rhythms and harmonies strengthen and soothe.

How ever many griefs life confronts us with,
music will still be wonderful.

AN OUTBREAK OF KINDNESS

Isn't this what makes life bearable,
given freely, with compassion, with humility,
not expecting anything in return,
except the alleviation of another's burden?
Somewhere inside we are all Samaritans.
I know it doesn't seem so -
such is the enmity, the cruelties we are capable of,
such is the indifference, the antipathy, the hate
ascendant in the world.

Yet somewhere at this very moment
a nurse sits by the bed of a dying stranger offering comfort.

How is it we don't prize kindness more -
be it moral duty,
be it part of our human heritage?
Perhaps we fear its call, fear our own vulnerability,
valuing self reliance above all?
But in the temple of our hearts
kindness is our liturgy.
We know kindness, we know when we withhold it.
We know the delight of giving.
It doesn't take much to smile a greeting
to speak a few consoling words, to help when help is needed.

Can you think of anything more transforming
than an outbreak of kindness in the world?

IN SUCH TIMES

There will be times
when we feel alone, disconnected, lonely;
such heartache!
We are not meant to live this way we say.
Where are the eyes that
shine with affection?
Where are the arms that bind with love?
Where are the softly spoken words of comfort and kindness?

You are not alone.
The universe watches and waits;
waits longingly for your imagination
to reach out and claim your place in the world.
The whole kingdom of life waits to welcome you home.
And it doesn't matter what you believe;
at this very moment love is flowing towards you.
Open your heart,
be ready.

BARISTA BOY

I left a heart drawn
on a napkin in a coffee shop
hoping the sad barista boy
might find it and know
that some day love will find him waiting and
invest his life with meaning;
that some day
his heart will break open in delight
and like happy contagion infect his world.

THE RITUAL

A ritual of remembrance doesn't have to be elaborate:
a small cairn of gathered stones;
a circle drawn in the tide smoothed sand, where
the river, ever flowing, meets the ocean;
a ring of hag-stones;
a piece of bleached and sculptural driftwood
in which a tiny white whelk shell
has become lodged in a knot hole.

All can be an altar to loss.

We bring our grief
and lay it there.

Maybe two swans will heave their heavy bodies into the air
and like emissaries from some other light filled realm
carry away our sorrow.

PRODIGAL

If we should meet again, by chance say -
I don't know how this might happen,
but let's say it did, in some freak
transposition of time and space -
what would we say one to another?
Would we fall on each other
In love and joy?
Would I bring you home,
shower you with riches,
not ask one single sorrowful why,
just hold you tight to my grief wrecked heart,
my beautiful boy, and
know again the gladness of your
presence in the world?

Yes, oh yes. A thousand times yes.

For Gareth

A NOTE UNSEEN

I wish you could have waited
for me to say again
how much your life mattered.
Waited for the blessings
already bestowed on your unfolding life,
as on any life,
to someday be revealed.
Waited for enriching sun kissed
horizons to open to your sight.
Waited for the love out there in the world,
that at the very moment of your going
was searching for you.
Waited for the creative flame of your life to
surprise and delight you with its fierce illumination.
Waited in the darkness in the certainty the light would return.
Waited for me to say again and again
how much your life mattered.

For Gareth

WHY SO MANY YOUNG MEN

What impels us to live
when life lets us down -
when all expectations, desires, dreams
become nothing but unreachable illusions -
when our place in this life has little meaning -
when our life force dims in a gathering darkness -
when there is not enough hope to anchor us here?

There is no blame;
but let us be sure our young men
always walk in the light of their own promise -
in the joy of their vital masculinity -
in the beauty of their essential goodness -
let them know always they are loved
beyond measure -
let them know their place at the table
is already set and waiting.

629 young men took their own lives in the UK in 2020

BEAUITFUL BOY

Years dim the memory of the beautiful boy you were.
The sound of your voice replays so softly now
that I strain to hear you.

Yet sometimes you are so palpably close
I could reach out and touch you;
feel again the thin frame of your body.

Strange how that felt sense remains so strong.

There were never enough hugs.

For Gareth

THE ROTHKO ROOM

We spill in and settle,
drawn by the gentle luminosity.
People speak in reverent whispers,
sensing that in this room
something silent and sacred is immanently present.

On the walls the large canvases bearing
soft rectangular reds, mauves, blacks, quietly vibrate.
We stare deeply into them and
the cares of the world seem to momentarily cease,
as consciousness reaches out, finding there,
beyond the harrowed mind, a welcome peace.

Rothko Room Tate Modern

HOPPER'S GAZE

I don't know the narrative;
what narratives form in my imagination
are of the darker kind.
Like a film still,
the subjects wait to be spooled on -
ominously something has happened,
or is about to happen
just beyond the frame.
What is it in these paintings
that finds an echo in the chambers
of the human heart?
The melancholy,
the haunting loneliness, the alienation
of one always looking on, always apart?

Then there is the light,
always the light,
streaming in through the open window,
through the doorway,
a bright illuminated interior at night,
rays of hope that seem to invite us to
step into that radiance,
let it suffuse body and mind,
let it fill us with delight.

'There is a sort of elation about sunlight ....' Edward Hopper

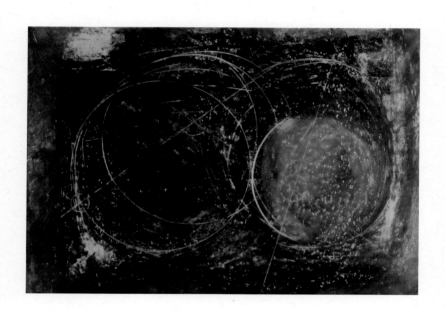

WHAT DO YOU THINK ABOUT WHEN YOU THINK ABOUT BLUE?

The immensity of a cloudless summer sky,
heavenly blue -
the flash of electric blue
as a kingfisher darts from a river bank -
a sweet smelling coverlet of bluebells in a May wood -
the blue Madonna -
the deep blue eyes of a lover
in which you once lost & found yourself -
blue jeans -
old bluesmen keeping on keeping on -
our lonely blue planet
spinning through darkly expanding space -
the slow burning of a blue sapphire -
Picasso's blue period
when the blue pigments of his deepest longings
set down his heart's sorrows.
Yes,
and yet
I do not know
of any colour in the world
that seeps into the soul like indigo,
bringing such calm, such peace, such stillness.

ENDPIECE

ENOUGH

Enough. These few words are enough.
If not these words, this breath.
If not this breath, this sitting here.

This opening to life
we have refused
again and again
until now.

Until now.

From David Whyte's 'Where Many Rivers Meet'
©Many Rivers Press

PERMISSIONS

Extract from Thich Nhat Hanh's, Touching Piece (1992) is printed with kind permission of Parallax Press, Berkeley USA

'Black Wood' from Robert Macfarlane's The Wild Places (2007) is printed with kind permission of the author and Granta Books, London.

David Whyte's, Enough, from Where Many Rivers Meet (1990) is printed with kind permission of Many Rivers Press, Langley, WA USA www.davidwhyte.com

Peter Watkins is a Suffolk Poet living close to the Stour estuary. He is a retired psychiatric nurse and co-founder of Inside Out Community, an award winning arts in mental health charity based in Ipswich. The landscape of the Stour valley provides the inspiration and motifs for many of his poems. As the American poet Mary Oliver once said 'the door to the woods is also the door to the temple' so it is for this poet, where every field track, every river path may become a portal to the beauty and wonder of nature. The poems in this, his second collection, were written during the Covid Pandemic of 2020/21 and reflect deeply on the consolations of the natural world. Seen through a wider lens they are an exploration of what it means to be human and our interconnection with the more than human world.

This beautifully produced and illustrated book is almost overwhelming in its simplicity. The poems lack all poetic pretensions but the images and thoughts sparkle like dew on the grass in the early morning. Each of these poems is the fruit of one man's solitary walks and meditations and are unlike any other poetry in their immediacy. And how beautifully Carol's artwork enhances the words.

James Roose Evans, author of: Older - A Thought Diary; Inner Journey Outer Journey; A Life Shared; and Blue Remembered Hills.

2022

Carol Lawrence is a multidisciplinary artist, poet and book publisher. Her work has been exhibited in group and solo exhibitions in Cornwall, East Anglia, London and Internationally.

Drawing her inspiration from observed forms and patterns, archways, standing stones, sky, sea and land, Carol Lawrence's paintings are largely abstract impressionistic in nature. The use of colour plays an integral part in her work, not for naturalistic purposes, but to imbue the paintings with energy, mystical and spiritual power so that the viewer becomes involved in a meditational engagement with the painting. She is a self taught artist.
www.carollawrence.co.uk
www.//instagram.com/carollawrenceartist

Eye Wild Books publishes small print run poetry and art books from our garden studio on the glorious bird strewn shoreline of the Stour Estuary, in Suffolk. Combined with our passion for poetry and art and our attention to detail we are able to produce, for the individual poet or artist, a book of fine quality that is both beautiful to hold and behold.